W9-BSX-693

The New How To Pick & Strum The Ukulele Book One

ISBN: 0-917822-24-2

Published In Hawaii By:
HEEDAY'S PUBLICATIONS
94-1211D Kipa'a Place
Waipahu, Hawaii 96797

How To Tune Your Ukulele

IF YOU HAVE A PIANO OR UKULELE PITCH PIPE, YOU CAN USE THEM TO TUNE YOUR. UKE. SIMPLY PLAY THE APPROPRIATE PITCHES ON EITHER THE PIANO OR THE PIPES AND MATCH YOUR STRINGS.

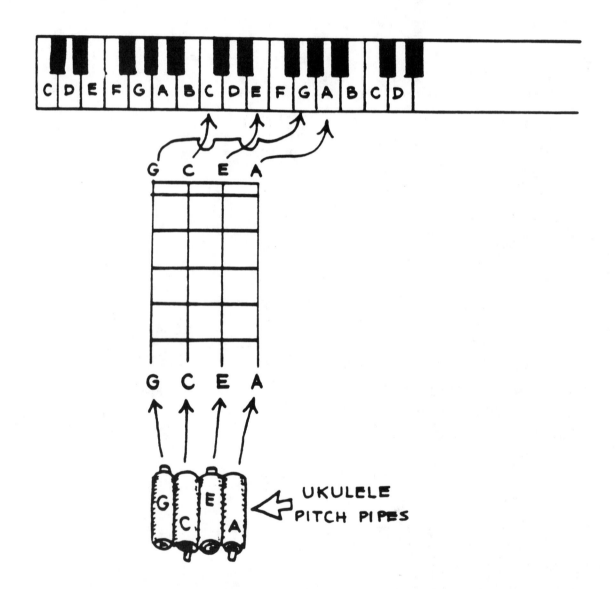

IF YOU HAVE NEITHER PIANO NOR PITCH PIPES, TUNE BY "EAR" AS SHOWN ON PG. 3.

Tuning By "Ear"

STEP 1: TUNE THE "A" OR BOTTOM STRING TO A COMFORTABLE PITCH. DON'T PITCH IT TOO LOW SINCE THE OTHER STRINGS MUST BE TUNED IN RELATION TO IT.

STEP 2: HOLD THE OTHER STRINGS AT THE FRETS INDICATED & TIGHTEN OR LOOSEN THE STRINGS TO MATCH THE OPEN "A" STRING.

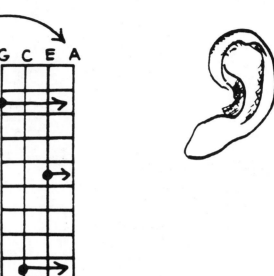

STEP 3: DOUBLE-CHECK YOUR TUNING BY MATCHING PITCHES IN 1, 2, 3 ORDER. THESE PAIRS MUST SOUND THE SAME.

STEP 4: CHECK ALSO WITH THE "DO-RE-MI" SCALE. DOES EVERY NOTE SOUND RIGHT?

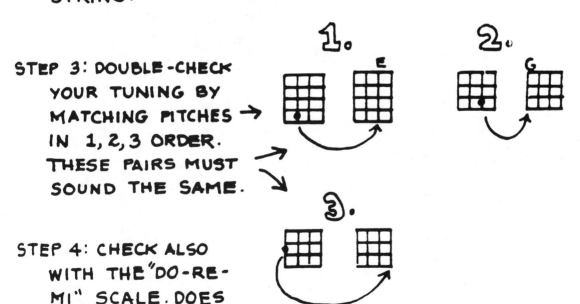

DO   RE   MI   FA   SO   LA   TI   DO

3

IF YOU TUNE YOUR TOP STRING ONE OCTAVE LOWER
THAN STANDARD TUNING, HOLD THE FIFTH FRET OF THE
TOP STRING & MATCH IT TO THE OPEN "C" STRING--
ASSUMING THE LATTER IS ALREADY TUNED.

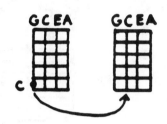

How To Hold Your Ukulele

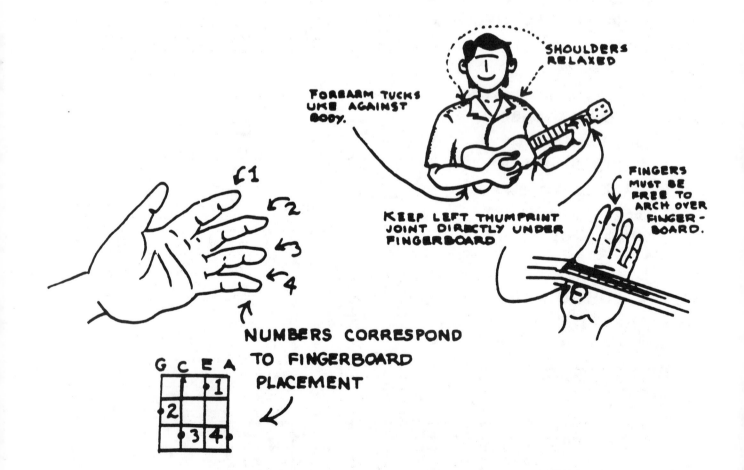

SHOULDERS
RELAXED

FOREARM TUCKS
UKE AGAINST
BODY.

KEEP LEFT THUMBPRINT
JOINT DIRECTLY UNDER
FINGERBOARD

FINGERS
MUST BE
FREE TO
ARCH OVER
FINGER-
BOARD.

NUMBERS CORRESPOND
TO FINGERBOARD
PLACEMENT

Beginning To Read Music

TO DEVELOP A WIDER REPERTOIRE OF SONGS, THE ABILITY TO READ AT LEAST SOME BASIC MUSIC IS VERY HELPFUL. LET'S COVER SOME BASICS:

The group of five lines is called a "STAFF".

NAMES OF SPACES

NAMES OF LINES

E C A F

F D B G E

The staff is divided into equal time units by vertical lines. The units are called "MEASURES".

MEASURE 1   MEASURE 2   MEASURE 3, ETC.

The clef sign is shown at the beginning of the staff. Ukulele music is written in the "TREBLE CLEF".
It is also known as the "G-CLEF" since its tail curls around the "G" line.

F D B G E

Timing is indicated by numerical indicators called "TIME SIGNATURES" usually placed at the beginning of the staff immediately after the clef sign.

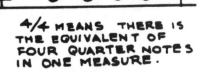

4/4 MEANS THERE IS THE EQUIVALENT OF FOUR QUARTER NOTES IN ONE MEASURE.

"C" IS THE SAME AS 4/4 TIME.

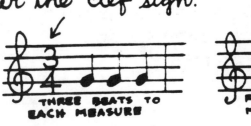

TWO BEATS TO EACH MEASURE

THREE BEATS TO EACH MEASURE

FOUR BEATS TO EACH MEASURE

THIS IS A QUARTER NOTE. ⟶ ♩ = ONE BEAT

THIS IS A HALF NOTE. ⟶ ♩ = TWO BEATS

THIS IS A WHOLE NOTE. ⟶ O = FOUR BEATS

THE QUARTER NOTE COMES IN TWO VERSIONS. THE STEMS MAY BE UP OR DOWN AS SHOWN HERE. ⟶

THE SAME HOLDS TRUE FOR HALF NOTES AND EIGHTH NOTES WHICH YOU'LL BE COVERING IN THIS BOOK. ⟶

A GROUP OF TWO OR MORE EIGHTH NOTES MAY BE JOINED BY A LINE OR STAND INDIVIDUALLY ALONE. ⟶

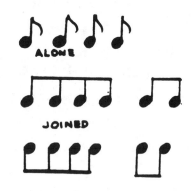

A DOT ADDED TO A NOTE INCREASES ITS VALUE BY ½ ITS VALUE.

EVERY SPACE AND EVERY LINE ON THE STAFF HAS AN ALPHABETICAL NAME.

QUESTION: HOW LONG IS ONE FULL
BEAT IN 4/4, 2/4 OR 3/4 TIME?

ANSWER ONE: IF YOU USE A TIME-BEATING
DEVICE CALLED THE METRONOME, THE INTERVAL
BETWEEN ONE TICK TO THE NEXT IS ONE
BEAT.

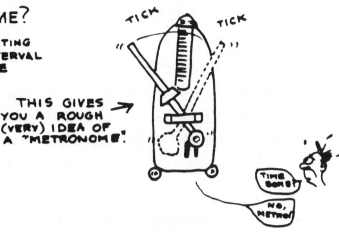

THIS GIVES
YOU A ROUGH
(VERY) IDEA OF
A "METRONOME"!

ANSWER TWO: ONE "BLUPITY BLURP"
OF YOUR HEARTBEAT.

ANSWER THREE: ONE DOWN AND UP
(OR UP AND DOWN) MOVEMENT OF THE
FOOT PROVIDED IT'S DONE IN AN EVEN
SMOOTH RHYTHM. THIS IS THE METHOD
FOLLOWED IN THIS BOOK.

1.

STARTING
POSITION

2.

FOOT MOVES
DOWN AND ZAPS
FLOOR. THIS IS
THE FIRST HALF
OF THE BEAT.

THE FULL BEAT IS
COMPLETED WHEN
THE FOOT RISES
BACK TO THE ORIGINAL
STARTING POSITION.

DON'T SKIP
PRACTICE JUST
BECAUSE YOU HAVE
A SLIGHT COLD!
JUST KEEP YOUR
TIMING FOOT WARM
AND KEEP PLAYING.

QUESTION: HOW DO I APPLY MY FOOT TIMING TO
MY PICKING PRACTICE?

ANSWER: FOLLOW THE UKE DIAGRAMS. PICK
ONLY THE STRINGS INDICATED BY
"X"'S, AS SHOWN HERE. ———

PICK
ONLY
THIS

TO ADD TIMING, BEAT OUT THE FOOT
RHYTHM FOR EACH NOTE. MAKE SURE YOUR
FOOT GOES UP AND DOWN EVENLY; OTHERWISE,
YOUR TIMING WILL BE ERRATIC! IF YOU USE
BOTH YOUR FOOT AND A METRONOME, YOUR
TIMING WILL BE BETTER. PRACTICE THE BASIC
PICKING EXERCISE ON THE NEXT PAGE.

ALMOST ANYONE CAN PICK WELL, IF S/HE PUTS IN A FEW MINUTES A DAY TO PRACTICE.

To start, use your right thumb to pick the top two strings and the right index finger to pick the bottom two strings. Later, you can try other picking techniques, but for now stick with the THUMB-INDEX PICKING METHOD.

The thumb picks in a downwise direction, and the index finger in an upward.

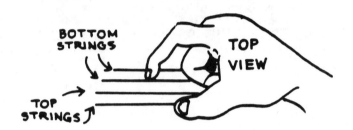

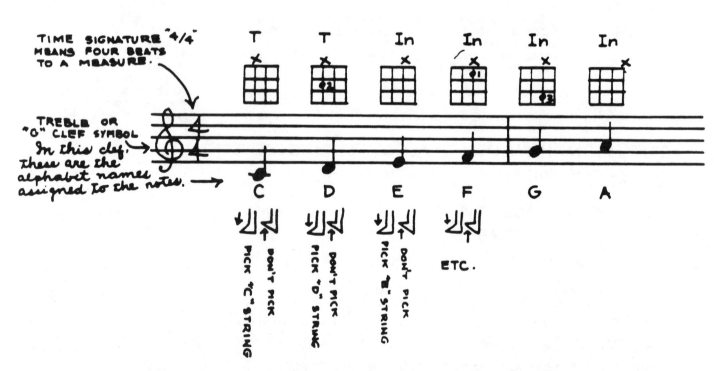

YOU PICK ON THE FIRST HALF OF THE QUARTER NOTE (AS YOUR FOOT HITS THE FLOOR & THEORETICALLY LET THE SOUND SUSTAIN ITSELF AS YOUR FOOT RISES.

Notes On The 1st Or "A" String

- SING THE NAME OF EACH NOTE YOU PICK.
- KEEP STRICT TIME WITH FOOT.

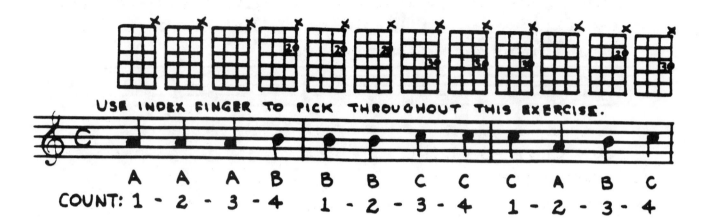

USE INDEX FINGER TO PICK THROUGHOUT THIS EXERCISE.

A A A B   B B C C   C A B C
COUNT: 1 - 2 - 3 - 4   1 - 2 - 3 - 4   1 - 2 - 3 - 4

Exercise

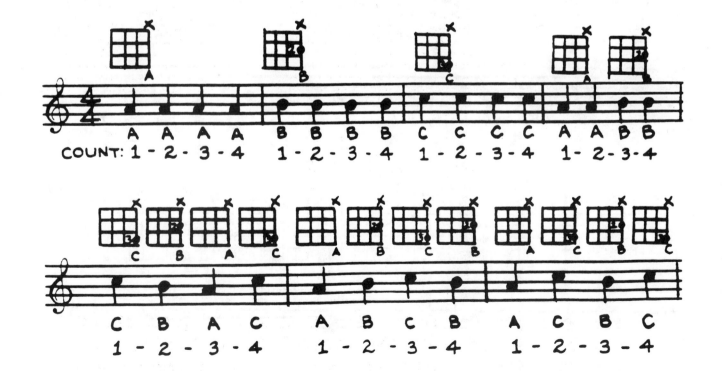

A A A A B B B B C C C C A A B B
COUNT: 1 - 2 - 3 - 4   1 - 2 - 3 - 4   1 - 2 - 3 - 4   1 - 2 - 3 - 4

C B A C   A B C B   A C B C
1 - 2 - 3 - 4   1 - 2 - 3 - 4   1 - 2 - 3 - 4

- SING THE NAME OF EACH NOTE YOU PICK.
- KEEP STRICT TIME WITH YOUR FOOT.

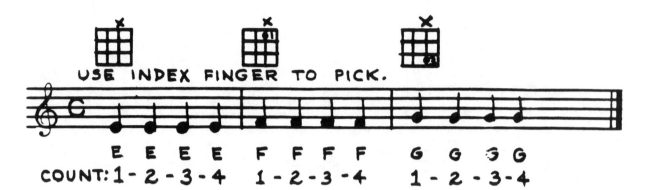

USE INDEX FINGER TO PICK.

E E E E F F F F G G G G
COUNT: 1 - 2 - 3 - 4 1 - 2 - 3 - 4 1 - 2 - 3 - 4

Exercise

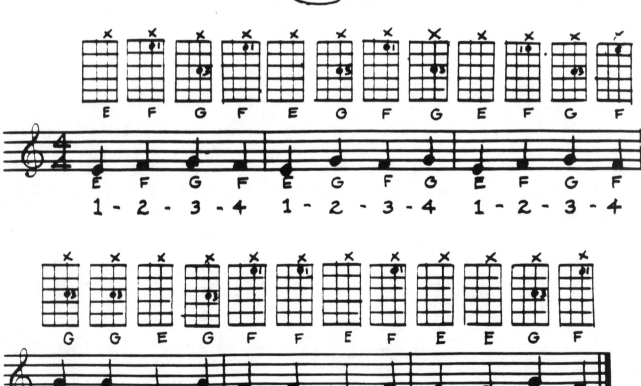

E F G F E G F G E F G F
E F G F E G F G E F G F
1 - 2 - 3 - 4 1 - 2 - 3 - 4 1 - 2 - 3 - 4

G G E G F F E F E E G F
G G E G F F E F E E G F
1 - 2 - 3 - 4 1 - 2 - 3 - 4 1 - 2 - 3 - 4

Combining 1st & 2nd Strings

- SING THE NAME OF EACH NOTE YOU PICK.
- USE INDEX FINGER TO PICK.

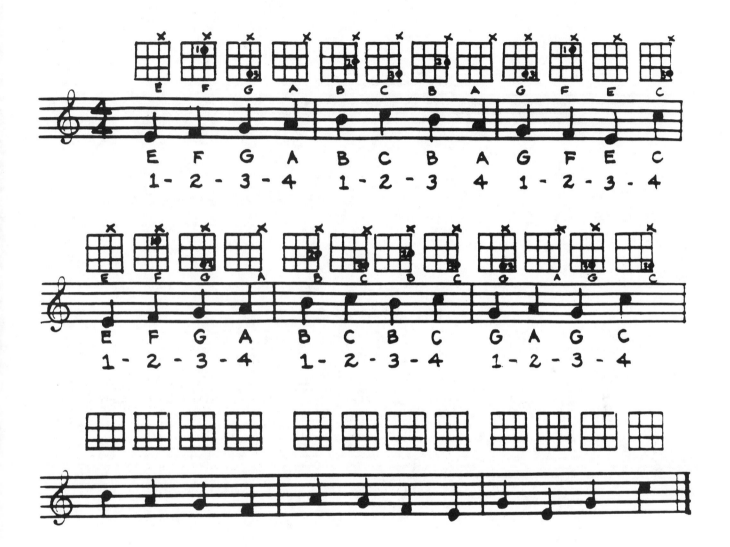

PRACTICE THIS PAGE UNTIL YOU CAN PLAY IT WITHOUT HESITATION OR ERROR. THEN WITHOUT LOOKING AT THE TOP TWO ROWS, FILL IN THE CORRECT FINGERINGS AND NOTE NAMES IN LINE 3 ABOVE. (Notice uke diagrams + names were left blank in Line 3.)

Notes On The 3rd Or "C" String

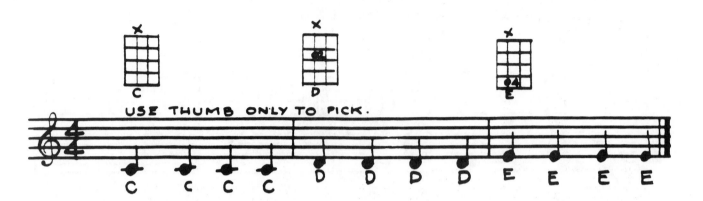

USE THUMB ONLY TO PICK.

C C C C D D D D E E E E

This lesson will give your little finger a good stretching. The average beginner has difficulty with the 4th finger so early practice is essential.

Exercise

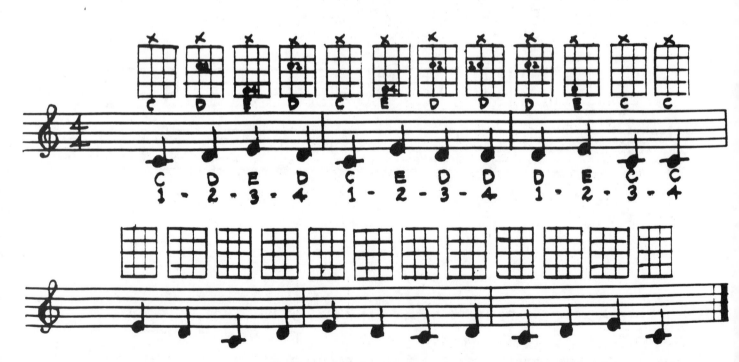

C D E D C E D D D E C C
1 - 2 - 3 - 4   1 - 2 - 3 - 4   1 - 2 - 3 - 4

WRITE IN THE FINGERINGS FOR THE LAST ROW.

Notes On The 4th Or "G" String

- IF YOU USE A LOW TOP "G" STRING, STUDY THE BOTTOM LINE. ( )

- USE THUMB TO PICK.

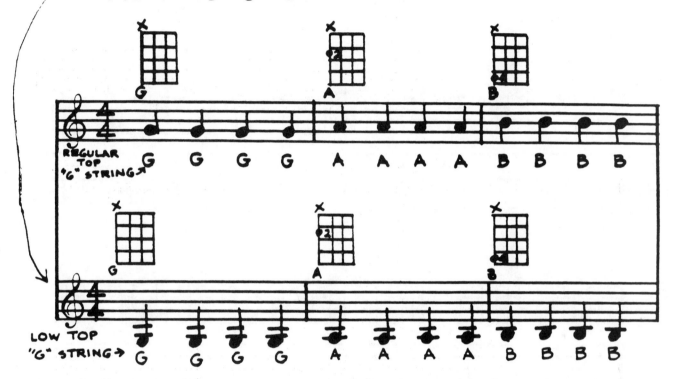

THE LOW NOTES WILL NOT BE EMPHASIZED IN THIS BOOK. HOWEVER, TO ACCOMMODATE THE LOW "G"-TUNED UKERS, THE TOP "G" STRING AS AN OPEN STRING WILL BE AVOIDED. INSTEAD, USE THE 3RD FRET OF THE 2nd OR "E" STRING FOR THE "G" NOTE.

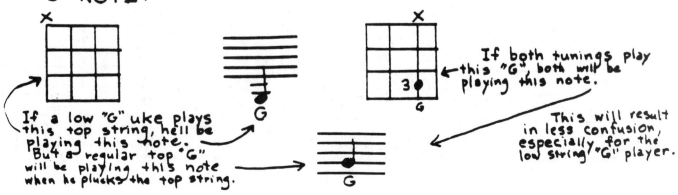

If a low "G" uke plays this top string, he'll be playing this note. But a regular top "G" will be playing this note when he plucks the top string.

If both tunings play this "G", both will be playing this note.

This will result in less confusion, especially for the low string "G" player.

THIS IS YOUR "DEBUT" INTO ALL-STRINGS
PLUCKING OR PICKING. REMEMBER TO USE
YOUR THUMB TO PICK TOP TWO STRINGS AND
INDEX FOR THE BOTTOM TWO STRINGS!

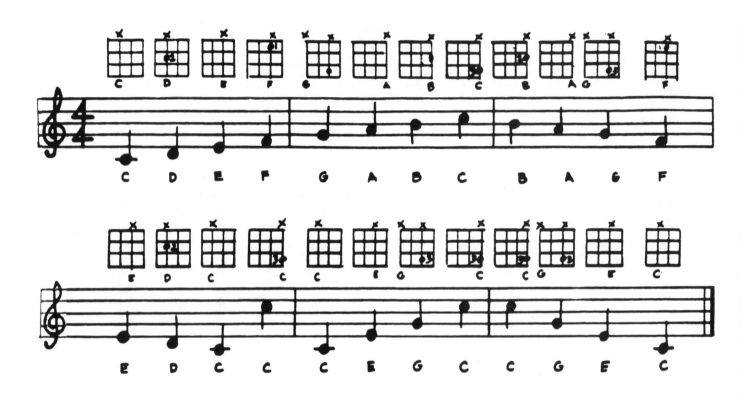

WHEN YOU CAN PLAY THE ABOVE BLINDFOLDED, TAKE
OFF THE BLINDFOLD & PLAY THE BELOW "BLIND" (SANS
FINGERING & LETTER NAMES). FILL IN DIAGRAMS.

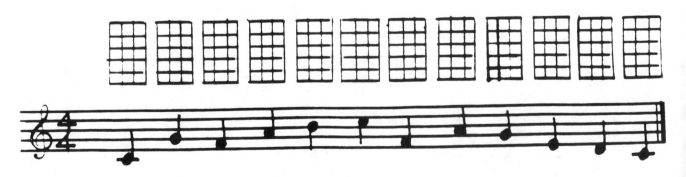

Your First Pickin' Solo

- PICK THE MELODY
- USE CORRECT FINGERS!
- ONCE YOU LEARN THE MELODY, SING AS YOU PICK.

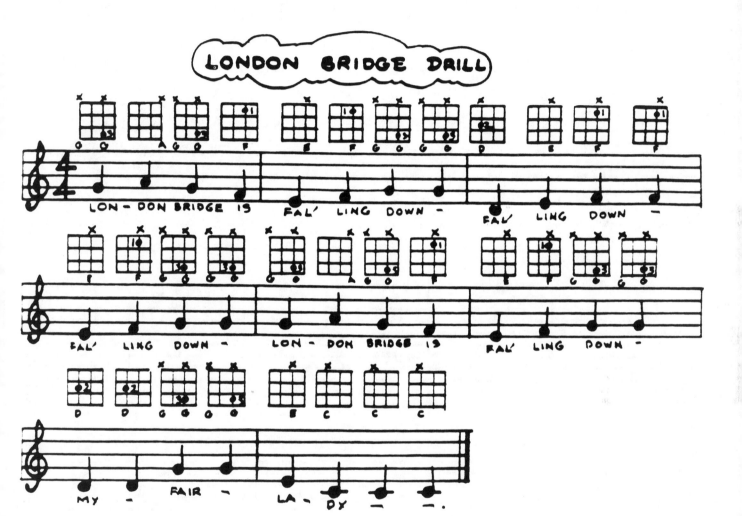

LONDON BRIDGE DRILL

LON - DON BRIDGE IS FAL' LING DOWN - FAL' LING DOWN -

FAL' LING DOWN - LON - DON BRIDGE IS FAL' LING DOWN -

MY - FAIR - LA - DY - -.

IF YOUR FIRST PICKIN' SOLO TURNED YOU ON, SHIFT YOUR FOOT INTO A STOMP AND PICK IT AGAIN! (Discretion advised if you have fussy neighbors-- especially downstairs)

STOMP STOMP
1 2. R 3.
HEEL HITS FLOOR

Review Page

LET'S SEE WHAT YOU HAVE LEARNED SO FAR.

1. PLAY THE FOLLOWING EXERCISE "BLIND" (WITHOUT PREMARKING THE DIAGRAMS) FIRST.

2. IF YOU GET STUCK, GO BACK TO PREVIOUS PAGES AND REPRACTICE. THEN COME BACK AND PLAY THIS PAGE AGAIN.

3. IF CONVINCED THAT YOU PLAYED IT THE MOST EFFICIENT WAY POSSIBLE, MARK THE FINGERING FOR EACH DIAGRAM. INCLUDE X'S ABOVE. & THE NAME OF EACH BELOW.

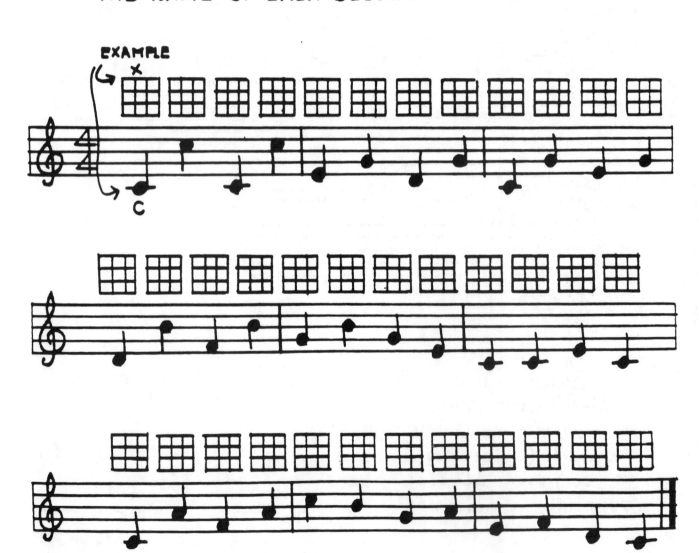

How To Play Half Notes And Whole Notes

To Play this:

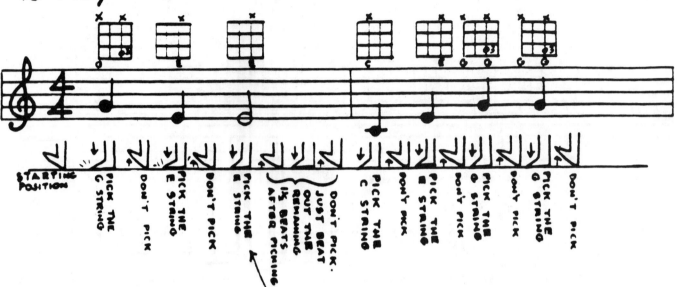

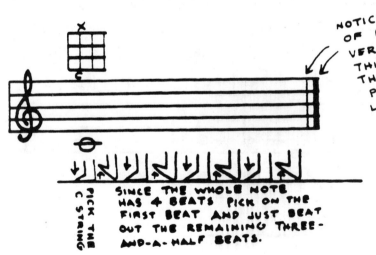

NOTICE COMBINATION OF DARK & LIGHT VERTICAL BARS. THIS MEANS IT'S THE END OF A PIECE OR SONG. LOOK FOR IT IN ALL SONGS.

SINCE THE WHOLE NOTE HAS 4 BEATS PICK ON THE FIRST BEAT AND JUST BEAT OUT THE REMAINING THREE-AND-A-HALF BEATS.

THIS PAGE IS A SHORT ONE BECAUSE IT IS IMPORTANT THAT YOU TAKE ALL THE TIME NECESSARY TO MASTER THE LESSON ON THIS PAGE.

LIGHTLY ROW

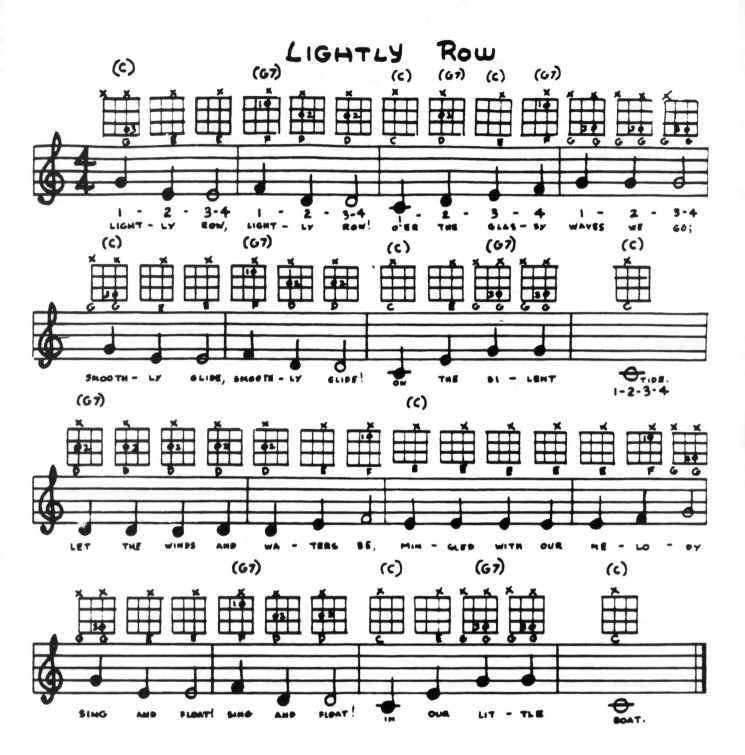

1. Play one line at a time.

2. On halfnotes, pick on the first half of the beat and merely beat out the remaining 1½ beats with your foot. Same for the whole notes except that you hold for 3½ beats after picking.

3. The letters in parentheses are chord names in case someone wants to accompany you. You can record your picking on a tape recorder and then practice accompanying yourself when you learn how to hold the C and G7 Chords.

TWINKLE TWINKLE

(Try the second line without looking at the diagrams above.)

Twin-kle, Twin-kle, Lit-tle Star, how I won-der what you are.

Up a-bove the world so high, like a dia-mond in the sky

When the eve-ning sun is set And the grass with dew is wet,

Then I see your lit-tle light, Twinkle, twinkle all the nite.

1. Learn the tune as you pick the first time.
2. Sing the song as you pick the second time.
3. Strum the chords while you sing the third time.
4. Use your tape recorder to record your picking and practice strumming in time to it. If you have no recorder, have a friend accompany you or vice-versa.

OLD SMOKEY

This is a waltz and is written in 3/4 time. "3/4 time" means there is the equivalent of 3 quarter notes in one measure.

On top of Old Smo-key-, all co-vered with snow, I lost my true lo-ver —— come-a cour-tin' too slow-.

1. NOTICE THE "C" NOTE IN THE FIRST MEASURE. IT STANDS ALONE AND THOUGH THIS SONG IS WRITTEN IN 3/4 TIME, YOU MAY BE WONDERING WHY ONLY ONE NOTE IS IN THE FIRST MEASURE. THE "C" NOTE IN THIS CASE IS CALLED A "PICKUP" NOTE AND IS A DEVICE USED IN MANY SONGS. NOTICE ALSO THAT IN THE LAST MEASURE THERE ARE ONLY 2 BEATS INSTEAD OF THE REQUIRED 3 BEATS PER MEASURE. THE 2 BEATS AT THE END COMBINE WITH THE PICKUP NOTE AT THE BEGINNING TO COMPLETE THE REQUIRED 3 BEATS.

2. "TIES" ARE USED 4 TIMES. REMEMBER THAT THE TIED NOTES FUNCTION AS ONE NOTE WITH COMBINED VALUES. THUS, DON'T PICK THE NOTES SEPARATELY. PICK ON THE FIRST BEAT AND HOLD FOR THE REMAINDER OF THE COMBINED VALUES.

Review Fun

LET'S JOG YOUR MEMORY WITH THIS QUICKIE!

1.  ← THIS IS A _____ NOTE. IN 4/4 TIME, IT HAS __ BEATS.

2. WHICH OF THESE EQUALS ONE FULL BEAT IN 4/4 TIME? (CIRCLE)

(POSED BY TWO MODELS)

3.  ← THE GROUP OF FIVE LINES IN MUSIC IS CALLED (CIRCLE CORRECT ANSWER) A. THE POLE B. THE STAFF C. THE BAMBOO

4. IN MUSIC, 4/4 TIME IS THE SAME AS
   A. WALTZ TIME   B. "C" TIME   C. 2/4 TIME

5.

WHAT IS THE NAME OF THIS SONG? (EXCERPT)

How To Do The Basic Downstrum

NOW THAT YOU CAN PICK SINGLE NOTES, YOU ARE NOW READY TO ADD THE STRUM. THE PICKING WAS IMPORTANT TO BEGIN BECAUSE BEFORE YOU CAN SING OR STRUM A SONG YOU OBVIOUSLY MUST KNOW THE TUNE. PICKING TEACHES YOU THE MELODY LINE VIA SINGLE STRING.

LET'S START WITH THE BASIC DOWNSTRUM.

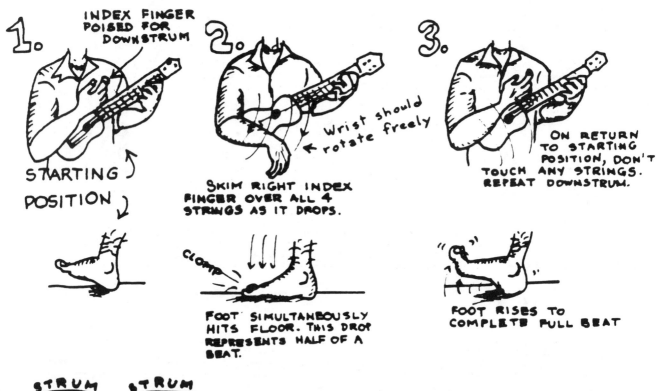

1. INDEX FINGER POISED FOR DOWNSTRUM

STARTING POSITION

2. Wrist should rotate freely

SKIM RIGHT INDEX FINGER OVER ALL 4 STRINGS AS IT DROPS.

FOOT SIMULTANEOUSLY HITS FLOOR. THIS DROP REPRESENTS HALF OF A BEAT.

3. ON RETURN TO STARTING POSITION, DON'T TOUCH ANY STRINGS. REPEAT DOWNSTRUM.

FOOT RISES TO COMPLETE FULL BEAT

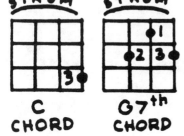

C CHORD

G7th CHORD

PRACTICE THESE CHORDS. IF AT FIRST YOU HAVE DIFFICULTY PLACING YOUR FINGERS, USE YOUR RIGHT HAND TO POSITION LEFT HAND FINGERS.

NOW LET'S STRUM. THE SLANT LINE EQUALS
ONE FULL BEAT. //// = 4 BEATS.

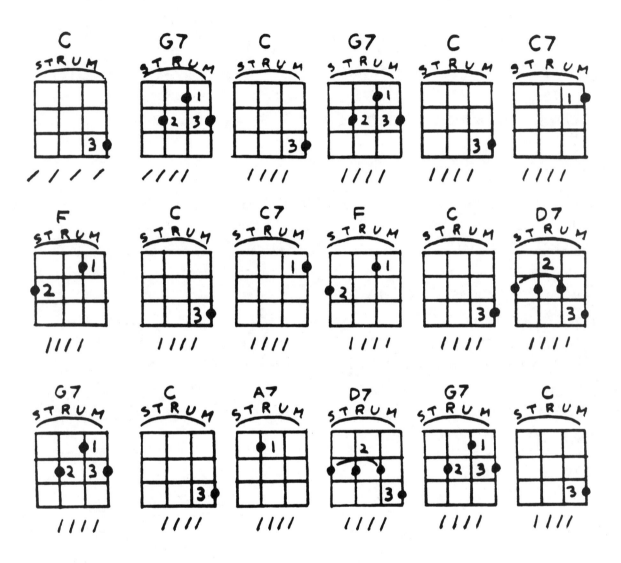

USE ONLY DOWNSTRUM FOR NOW. HOWEVER, EVERY
TIME YOU LEARN A NEW STRUMMING TECHNIQUE,
COME BACK TO THIS PAGE AND PRACTICE IT
WITH THESE CHORDS.

BE SURE TO MEMORIZE THESE CHORDS ONLY
BY REPEATED PRACTICE, NOT BY INTELLECTUALIZING!

Combining Pickin' & Strummin'

NOW THAT YOU CAN DO BASIC PICKING AND BASIC STRUMMING SEPARATELY, LET'S COMBINE THEM. THIS TECHNIQUE IS CALLED "PICK-STRUM".

AT THIS STAGE, THE PICK-STRUM MAY SOUND A BIT "STIFF" TO YOU BUT PRACTICE STEP-BY-STEP FOR NOW. EVENTUALLY, YOUR UKE CAN SOUND LIKE TWO-- ONE PICKING AND ONE STRUMMING!

HERE'S HOW TO "PICK-STRUM".

1. USE THE SINGLE-STRING PICKING SKILL TO PLAY THE MELODY (AS YOU DID FOR "LONDON BRIDGE", "LIGHTLY ROW", "TWINKLE, TWINKLE", & "OLD SMOKEY")

2. WHEN YOU COME TO ANY SUSTAINED NOTE OF TWO OR MORE BEATS (LIKE A HALF-NOTE, DOTTED HALF-NOTE OR A WHOLE NOTE), PICK THE NOTE AND, INSTEAD OF "RESTING" FOR THE REMAINING VALUE OF THAT SUSTAINED NOTE, HOLD THE CHORD FOR THAT NOTE AND STRUM OUT THE REMAINING VALUE.

FOR EXAMPLE:

A HALF NOTE ($\downarrow$) HAS 2 BEATS: PICK FOR THE FIRST BEAT ($\downarrow$) AND STRUM THE REMAINING BEAT (/).

A DOTTED HALF NOTE ($\downarrow$.) HAS 3 BEATS: PICK FOR THE FIRST BEAT ($\downarrow$) AND STRUM THE REMAINING 2 BEATS (//).

A WHOLE NOTE (O) HAS 4 BEATS: PICK FOR THE FIRST BEAT ($\downarrow$) AND STRUM THE REMAINING 3 BEATS (///).

COMBINING PICKIN' & STRUMMIN' (CONT'D.)

PICK-STRUM IS A VERY IMPORTANT SKILL IN UKE SOLO PLAYING. LET'S USE "LONG, LONG AGO" AS A STARTER. STUDY THIS PAGE WELL BEFORE YOU TACKLE THE FULLER SONG ON THE NEXT PAGE.

Long, Long Ago

CHORDS ARE
ENCLOSED IN
PARENTHESES.

• BE SURE TO PICK UPPER 2 STRINGS
  WITH THUMB, LOWER 2 WITH INDEX

NOTE
TREBLE
OR "G"
CLEF.

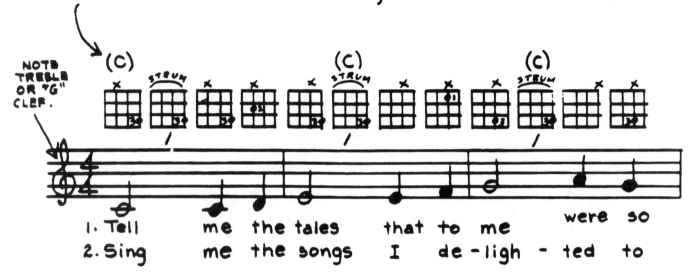

1. Tell me the tales that to me were so
2. Sing me the songs I de-ligh-ted to

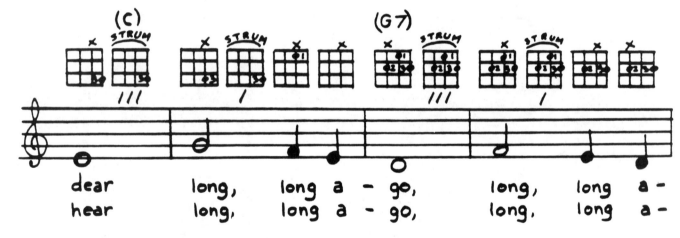

dear long, long a-go, long, long a-
hear long, long a-go, long, long a-

TWO DOTS BEFORE LIGHT
AND DARK TERMINAL LINES
MEANS TO REPEAT ALL BEFORE
THE DOTS (FROM THE BEGINNING).
SECOND THROUGH, END WITH
"AGO" IN BRACKET "2", NOT "1".

-go.   -go.

26

How To Strum "Long, Long Ago" In The Key Of "C"

- SLANT MARKS ARE ONE BEAT EACH (/).
- CHANGE CHORDS ON EXACT / MARK.

TELL ME THE TALES THAT TO ME WERE SO DEAR

LONG, LONG A-GO   LONG, LONG A-GO—.

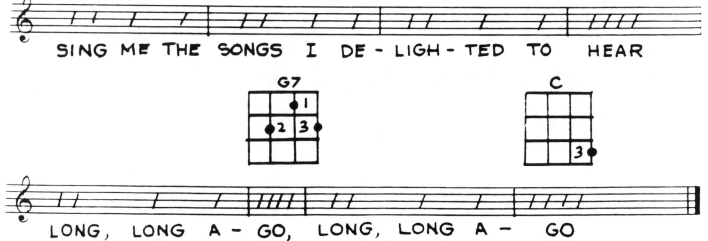

SING ME THE SONGS I DE-LIGH-TED TO HEAR

LONG, LONG A-GO, LONG, LONG A- GO

When The Saints Go Marching In

- REST ONE BEAT AT THE BEGINNING
- NOTICE "BOGUS" "C" CHORD IN ROW 1. → HOLD WITH RING FINGER.

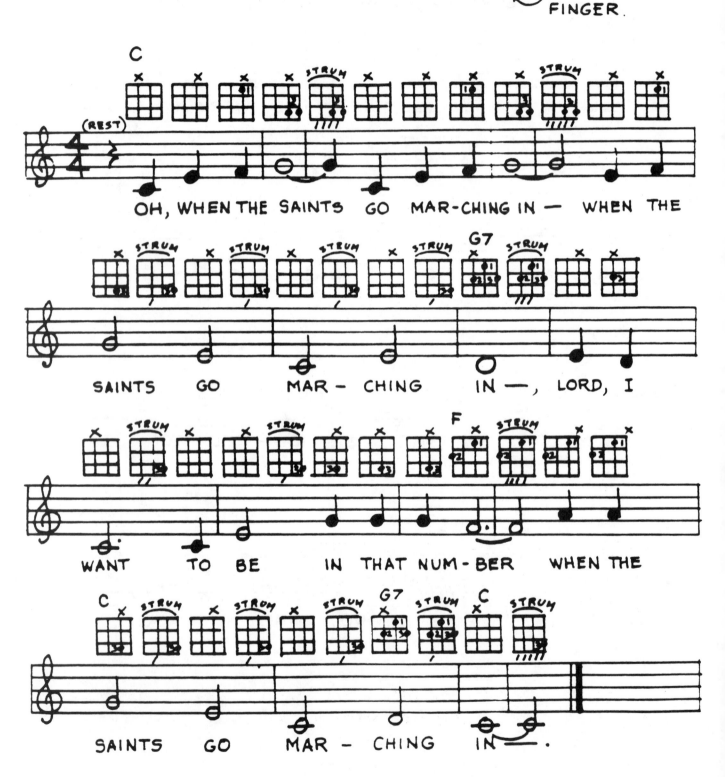

OH, WHEN THE SAINTS GO MAR-CHING IN — WHEN THE

SAINTS GO MAR-CHING IN —, LORD, I

WANT TO BE IN THAT NUM-BER WHEN THE

SAINTS GO MAR-CHING IN —.

*Strumming "When The Saints..."
In The Key Of "C"*

- START WITH BASIC DOWNSTRUM; ADD UP-AND-DOWN STRUM LATER.
- CHANGE CHORDS ON EXACT SYLLABLE AND SLANT (/) MARK.

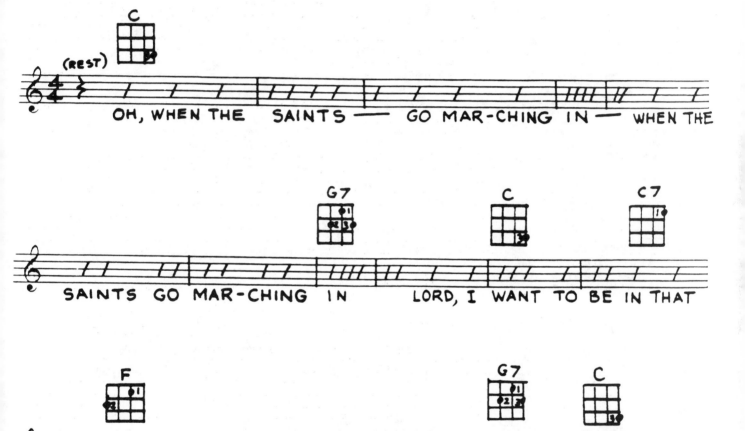

PRACTICE BOTH PAGES WELL (PAGE 28 AND THIS ONE). IF YOU HAVE A TAPE RECORDER, RECORD THE MELODY (PAGE 28) AND AS YOU PLAY YOUR PICK-STRUM BACK, YOU CAN PRACTICE YOUR STRUMMING.

How To Do The Up-And-Downstrum

1. MAINTAIN COMFORTABLE PRESSURE AGAINST UKE. INDEX FINGER POISED IN STARTING POSITION

STARTING POSITION OF FOOT

2. SKIM INDEX FINGER OVER ALL 4 STRINGS AS IT MOVES UP. ROTATE WRIST IN PROCESS.

3. ON THE DOWN FOOT DO A REGULAR BASIC DOWNSTRUM. SKIM INDEX FINGER DOWN ALL 4 STRINGS.

CLOMP

REPEAT STEPS 2 AND 3

• IN THE UP-AND-DOWN STRUM, THE DIRECTION OF YOUR STRUM (UP OR DOWN) IS THE SAME AS YOUR FOOT.

• MAKE YOUR DOWNSTRUMS SLIGHTLY HEAVIER THAN THE UPSTRUM.

• WHEN YOU CAN DO THIS COMFORTABLY WELL, GO BACK TO PAGE 23 AND PRACTICE STRUMMING THE CHORDS.

THEN USE THE UP-AND-DOWNSTRUM FOR "LONG, LONG AGO" (PG. 27) AND "WHEN THE SAINTS... (PG. 29).

How To Play Eighth Notes

• THE EIGHTH NOTE LOOKS LIKE THIS: ♪ OR 𝄾. IT LOOKS LIKE THE QUARTER NOTE EXCEPT THAT THE EIGHTH NOTES HAVE A TAIL EACH.

• IN 4/4 OR 3/4 TIME, THE EIGHTH NOTE (𝄾 OR ♪) EQUALS 1/2 (HALF-A) BEAT.

PICK UP YOUR UKE AND PRACTICE THE FOLLOWING:

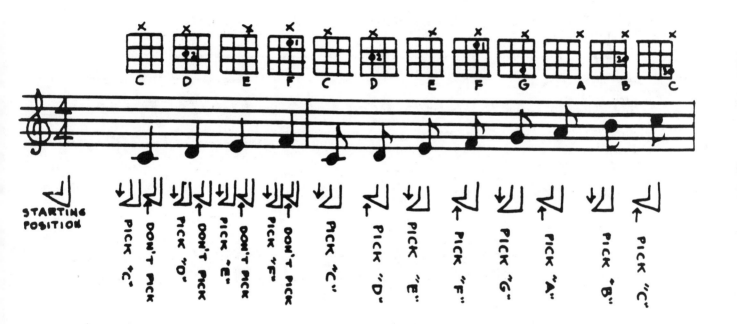

IN THE EXERCISE ABOVE, NOTICE THAT THE FIRST FOUR NOTES ARE QUARTER NOTES. THEREFORE, YOU PICK ON THE FIRST HALF OF EACH QUARTER NOTE AND REMAIN "SILENT" FOR THE SECOND HALF OF THE IT.

BUT IN PLAYING EIGHTH NOTES, YOU PICK ONCE ON THE FIRST HALF OF THE BEAT AND AGAIN ON THE SECOND HALF OF THE BEAT.

31

EIGHTH NOTES (CONT'D.)

EIGHTH NOTES CAN BE WRITTEN SINGLY OR MAY BE
JOINED BY A HORIZONTAL LINE AS SHOWN HERE.

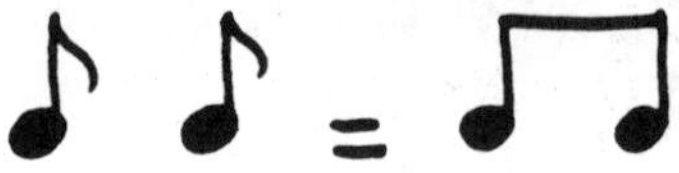

OTHER EXAMPLES ARE:

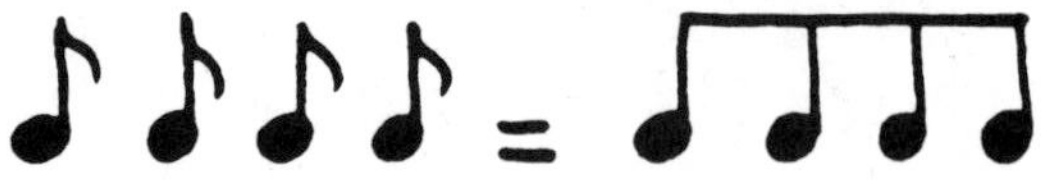

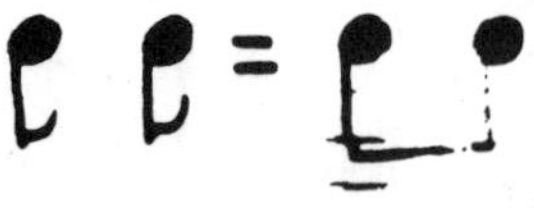

How To Count Quarter Notes & Eighth Notes

QUARTER NOTES ARE COUNTED:

COUNT: "ONE-AND" "TWO-AND "THREE-AND" "FOUR-AND"
NOTATION: 1 ↖   2 ↻   3 ↻   4 ↻

EIGHTH NOTES ARE COUNTED:

COUNT: "ONE-AND" "TWO-AND "THREE-AND" "FOUR-AND"
        1 ↻   2 ↻   3 ↻   4 ↻

COUNT "ONE-AND, TWO-AND..." AS YOU DO THE
FOOT TIMING EXERCISE ABOVE.

EIGHTH NOTES (CONT'D.)

HERE'S A ONE-NOTE PICKING PRACTICE TO SHARPEN YOUR QUARTER AND EIGHTH NOTES TIMING SENSE.

FILL IN THE SECOND ROW UNDER THE "C" NOTES. FOLLOW THE NOTATIONS UNDER THE FIRST ROW.

BE SURE YOU UNDERSTAND AND CAN PLAY ALL OF THE EIGHTH NOTE EXERCISES UP TO THIS PAGE BEFORE YOU PROCEED ANY FURTHER. IF YOU HAVE ANY MISUNDERSTOOD POINTS, GO BACK, REVIEW, AND PRACTICE WELL BEFORE RETURNING HERE.

THEN PRACTICE "SHORTNIN' BREAD" ON THE NEXT PAGE. ONE NOTE (NO PUN INTENDED) IN "SHORTNIN' BREAD" IS THAT EVEN IF YOU PICK ONLY ONE "X"'ED STRING, PRACTICE HOLDING THE CHORD FINGERING. FOR EXAMPLE,

EVEN IF THE "C" NOTE IS THE ONLY ONE YOU PICK, HOLD THE 3RD FINGER AT THE 3RD FRET. LATER, YOU'LL SEE WHY.

Shortnin' Bread

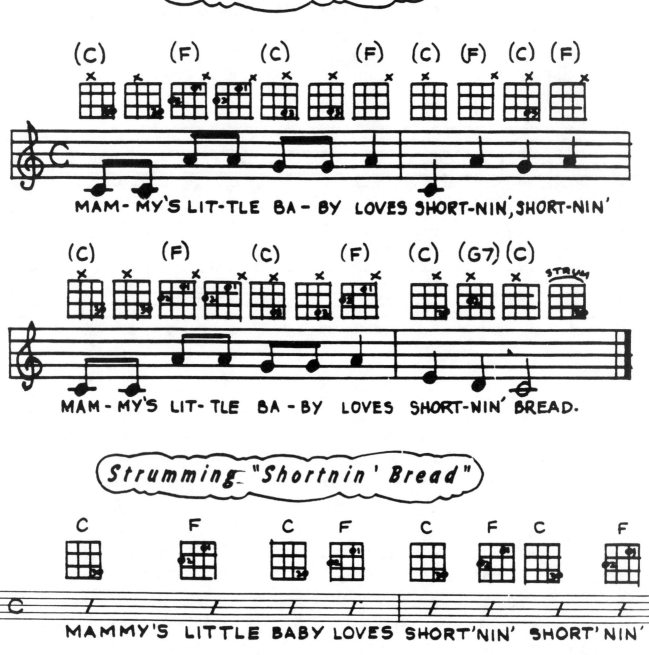

Strumming "Shortnin' Bread"

More Eighth Notes Practice

- WRITE THE NAME OF EACH NOTE BELOW IT.
- PLAY THIS EXERCISE

Caissons Go Rolling Along

(C)

O - VER HILL, O - VER DALE, AS WE HIT THE DUS - TY

(G7)   (C)

TRAIL AS THE CAIS - SONS GO ROL - LING A - LONG —. IN AND

OUT, HEAR THEM SHOUT, COUN - TER MARCH AND RIGHT A - BOUT AND THE

(G7)   (C)

CAI - SSONS GO ROL - LING A - LONG —.

Jingle Bells

TAKE A BREATHER FROM ALL THAT EIGHTH NOTE WORK WITH THIS ALL-TIME FAVORITE. REMEMBER TO USE THE CORRECT FINGERS FOR PICKING & CHORD HOLDING.

JIN-GLE BELLS, JIN-GLE BELLS, JIN-GLE ALL THE

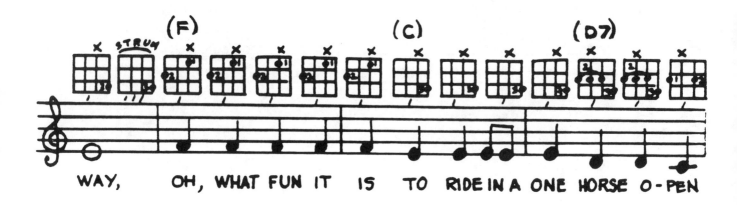

WAY, OH, WHAT FUN IT IS TO RIDE IN A ONE HORSE O-PEN

SLEIGH ———, JIN-GLE BELLS, JIN-GLE BELLS,

JIN-GLE ALL THE WAY, OH, WHAT FUN IT IS TO RIDE IN A

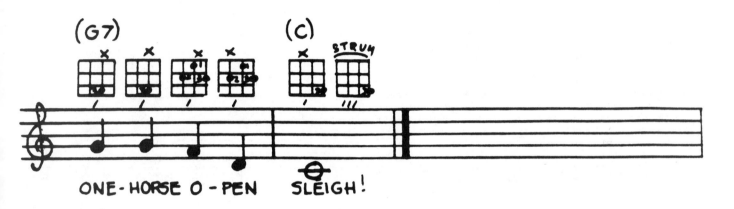

ONE-HORSE O-PEN SLEIGH!

AFTER YOU HAVE PICK-STRUMMED USING THE
BASIC "C" CHORD, PRACTICE SUBSTITUTING THE
ADVANCED "C" CHORD SHOWN BELOW. IT CAN
SIMPLIFY PICKING & STRUMMING.

BASIC
"C" CHORD

"C" CHORD
(ADVANCED
INVERSION)

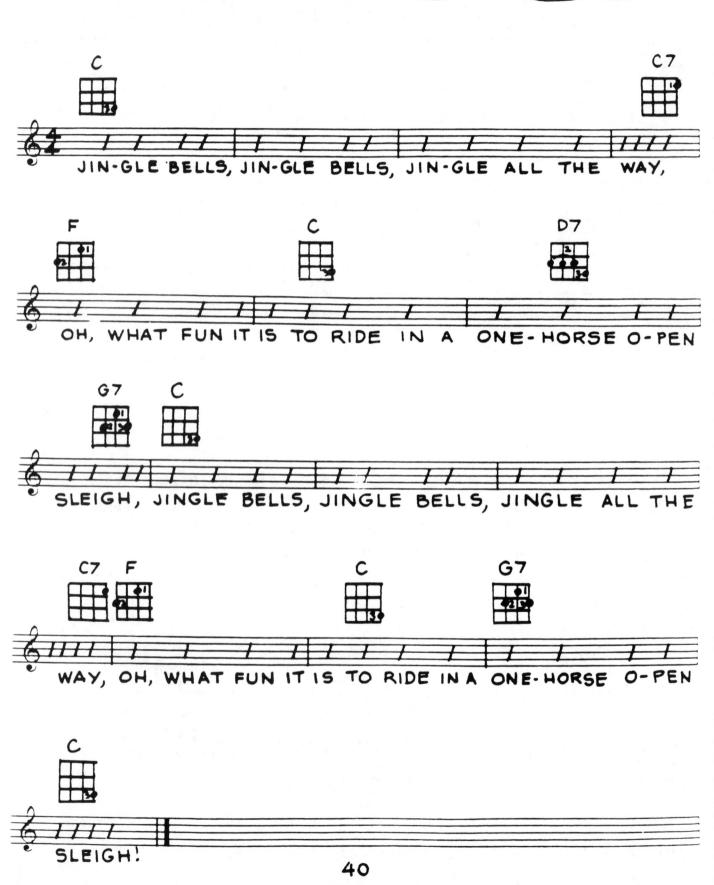

UP TO THIS POINT YOU HAVE BEEN PLAYING IN THE KEY OF "C MAJOR"-- THE KEY WITH NO SHARP (#) OR FLAT (b).

THE KEY OF "F" REQUIRES ONE FLAT. IT IS PLACED DIRECTLY ON THE "B" LINE OF THE STAFF.

THE FLAT ON THE "B" LINE MEANS THAT ALL NOTES THAT FALL ON THAT LINE ARE FLATTED EXCEPT WHEN NULLIFIED BY A NATURAL SIGN (♮) OR DOUBLE FLATS BEFORE THE PARTICULAR NOTE.

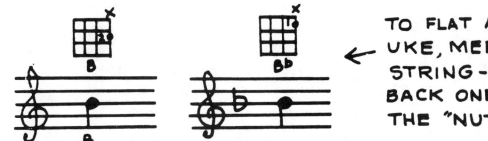

TO FLAT A NOTE ON THE UKE, MERELY MOVE THE STRING-HOLDING FINGER BACK ONE FRET TOWARD THE "NUT" OR PEGS.

OCCASIONALLY YOU MAY COME ACROSS A SONG WRITTEN IN THE KEY OF "F" THAT CONTAIN THE NATURAL (♮) SIGN ON THE Bb LINE. THAT MEANS YOU ARE TO PLAY THE NOTE IN ITS NATURAL STATE.

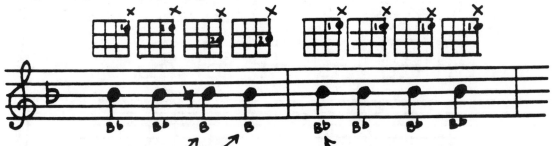

The natural sign changes the Bb to B only within the measure.

The natural sign becomes nullified in the next measure.

Clementine

HERE'S YOUR FIRST SOLO IN THE KEY OF "F" MAJOR.

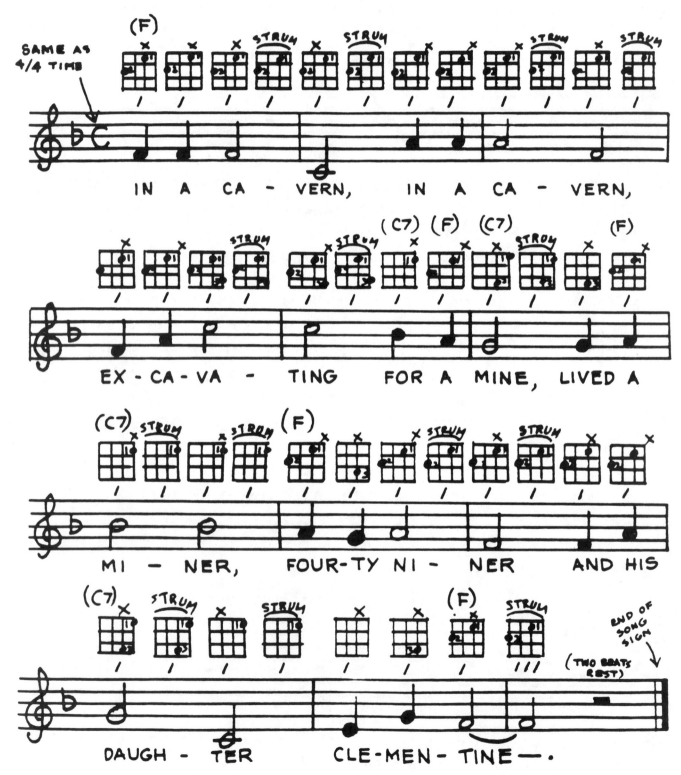

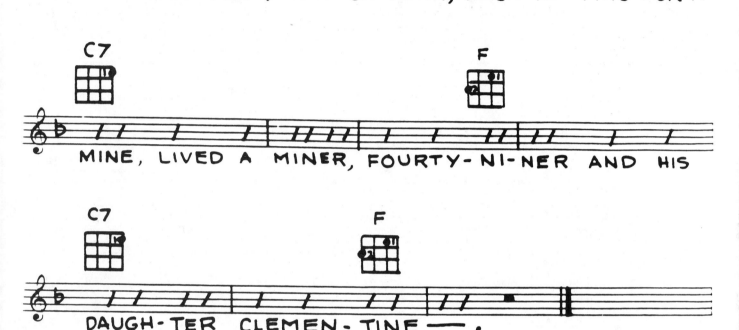

Additional Stanzas

2. Light she was and like a fairy
   And her shoes were number nine,
   Herring boxes without topses,
   Sandals were for Clementine.

Chorus (Repeat after every stanza)

Oh, my darling, Oh, my darling,
Oh, my darling Clementine!
You are lost and gone forever,
Dreadful sorry, Clementine!

3. Drove she ducklings to the water
   Every morning just at nine,
   Hit her foot against a splinter
   Fell into the foaming brine.

4. Ruby lips above the water
   Blowing bubbles soft and fine;
   As for me, I was no swimmer
   And I lost my Clementine.

5. How I missed her, how I missed her,
   How I missed my Clementine.
   Then I kissed her little sister
   And forgot dear Clementine.

43

Down In The Valley

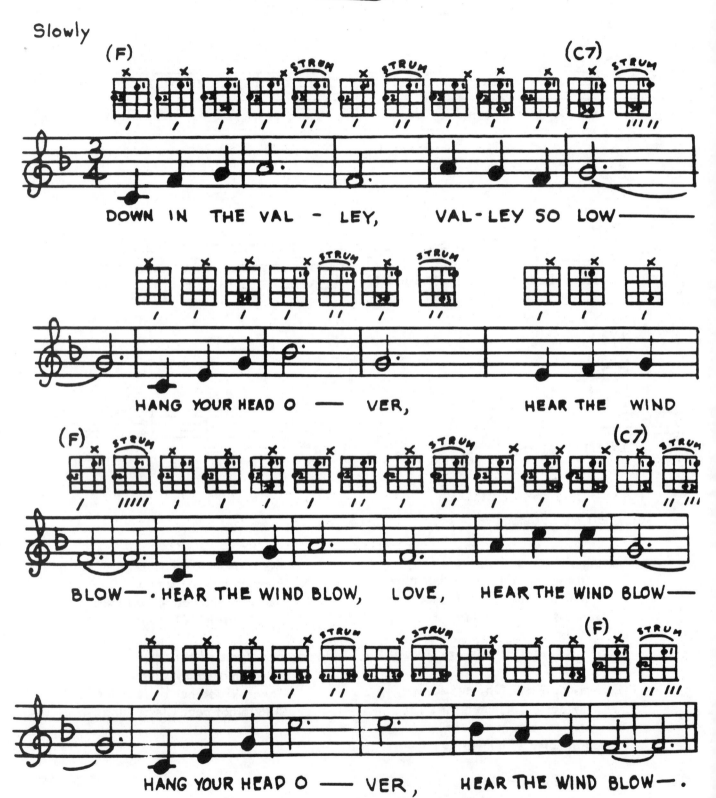

Slowly

DOWN IN THE VAL - LEY, VAL-LEY SO LOW —

HANG YOUR HEAD O — VER, HEAR THE WIND

BLOW —. HEAR THE WIND BLOW, LOVE, HEAR THE WIND BLOW —

HANG YOUR HEAD O — VER, HEAR THE WIND BLOW —.

Strumming "Down In The Valley" In The Key Of "F"

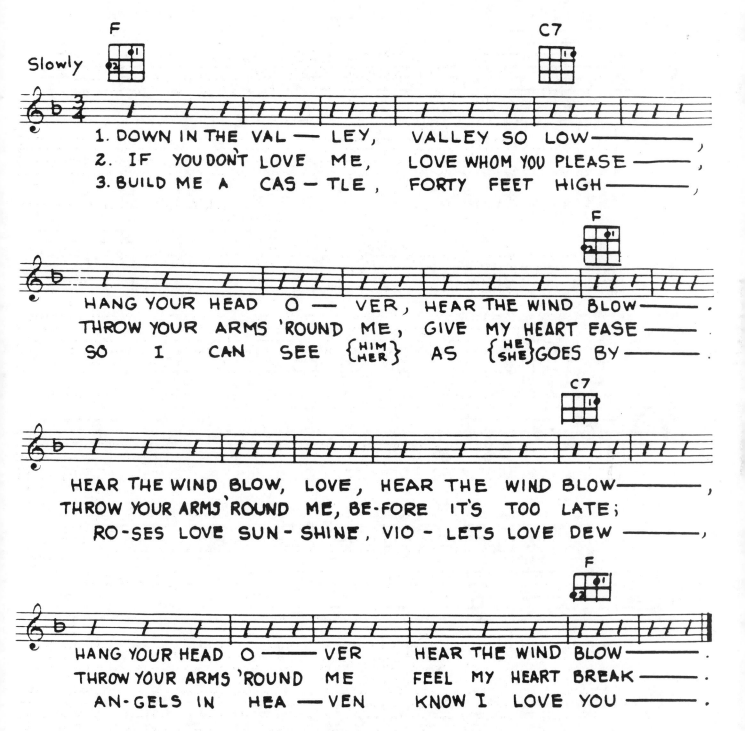

Home On The Range

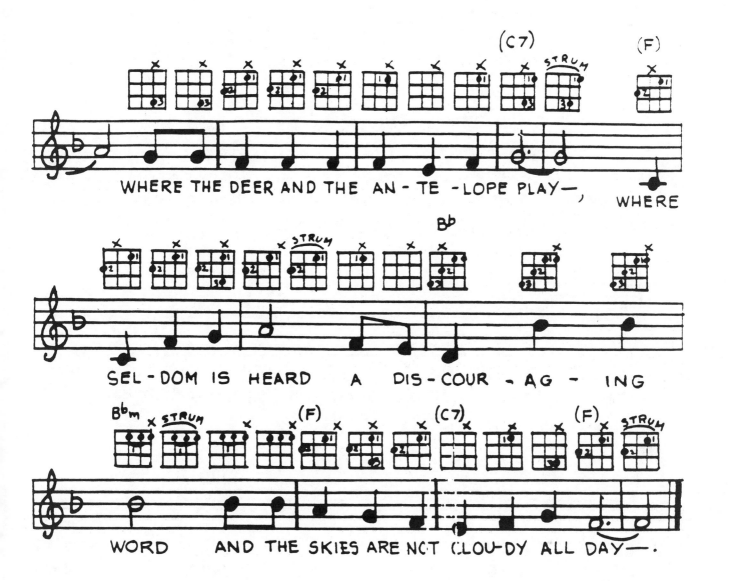

WHERE THE DEER AND THE AN-TE-LOPE PLAY—, WHERE

SEL-DOM IS HEARD A DIS-COUR-AG-ING

WORD AND THE SKIES ARE NOT CLOU-DY ALL DAY—.

HOLDING CHORDS WHILE PICKING SINGLE NOTES: YOU MAY HAVE DIFFICULTY HOLDING CHORDS WHILE KEEPING TRACK OF THE "X" STRING MELODY NOTES. YOU ALSO MAY BE ASKING WHY YOU MUST HOLD 3 OTHER STRINGS WHEN YOU PICK ONLY ONE STRING.

DEVELOPING THE ABILITY TO HOLD CHORDS WHILE PICKING WILL GREATLY SIMPLIFY ADVANCED SOLO PLAYING. IN CERTAIN "PHRASINGS" CHORD PICKING ARTS ARE MORE EFFICIENT. BUT IF TOO MUCH FOR YOU AT THIS STAGE, JUST PICK THE "X" STRINGS WITHOUT HOLDING THE CHORDS. HOLD CHORDS ONLY ON STRUMMING CUES IN SUCH SITUATIONS.

47

Strumming "Home On The Range" In The Key Of "F"

THE Bb CHORD OFTEN GIVES BEGINNERS SOME PROBLEMS. BE SURE HOLD ESPECIALLY THE TOP FINGERINGS (FIRST FRET) FIRMLY. ARCH YOUR MIDDLE AND RING FINGERS WELL SO THEY AVOID CONTACTING THE WRONG STRINGS.

1. OH, GIVE ME A HOME WHERE THE BUFFALO ROAM AND THE
2. HOW OF-TEN AT NIGHT WHEN THE HEAVENS ARE BRIGHT WITH THE

DEER AND THE ANTELOPE PLAY ——; WHERE SELDOM IS
LIGHT FROM THE GLITTERING STARS ——, HAVE I STOOD THERE A-

HEARD A DIS-COURAGING WORD AND THE SKIES ARE NOT
MAZED AND ASKED AS I GAZED IF THEIR GLO-RY EX-

Chorus

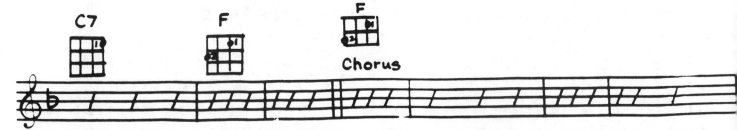

CLOUDY ALL DAY———;
CEEDS THAT OF OURS———?   HOME, HOME ON THE RANGE ——, WHERE THE

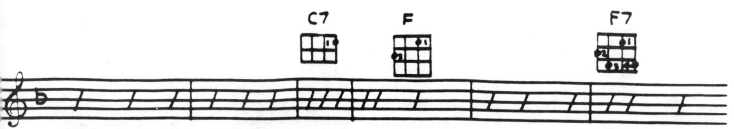

DEER AND THE ANTELOPE PLAY——, WHERE SELDOM IS HEARD A DIS-

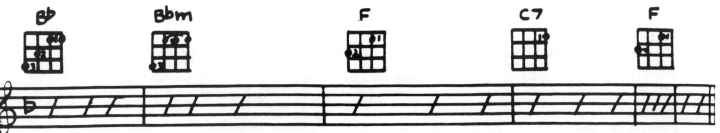

COURAGING WORD AND THE SKIES ARE NOT CLOUDY ALL DAY——.

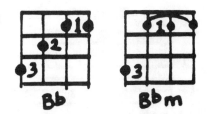

- NOTICE THAT I "SNUCK IN A "FANCY" CHORD CALLED
  "B♭m" OR "B-FLAT MINOR". IT WORKS IN NICELY,
  SOUNDWISE WHEN USED IN COMBO WITH THE BASIC
  B♭ CHORD.

- WHENEVER YOU SEE A LOWER CASE "m" AFTER A
  CHORD NAME, THAT MEANS IT'S A MINOR CHORD:
  EXAMPLES ARE B♭m = B♭ MINOR; Gm = G MINOR, ETC.

- WHENEVER YOU SEE A CAPITAL "M" AFTER AFTER A CHORD
  NAME, IT'S A MAJOR CHORD: "CM"="C MAJOR" "FM"="F
  MAJOR", ETC. HOWEVER, IN THE BASIC MAJOR CHORDS
  LIKE "C MAJOR" THE "M" IS USUALLY DELETED AND
  SIMPLY CALLED "C" CHORD.

49

Long, Long Ago

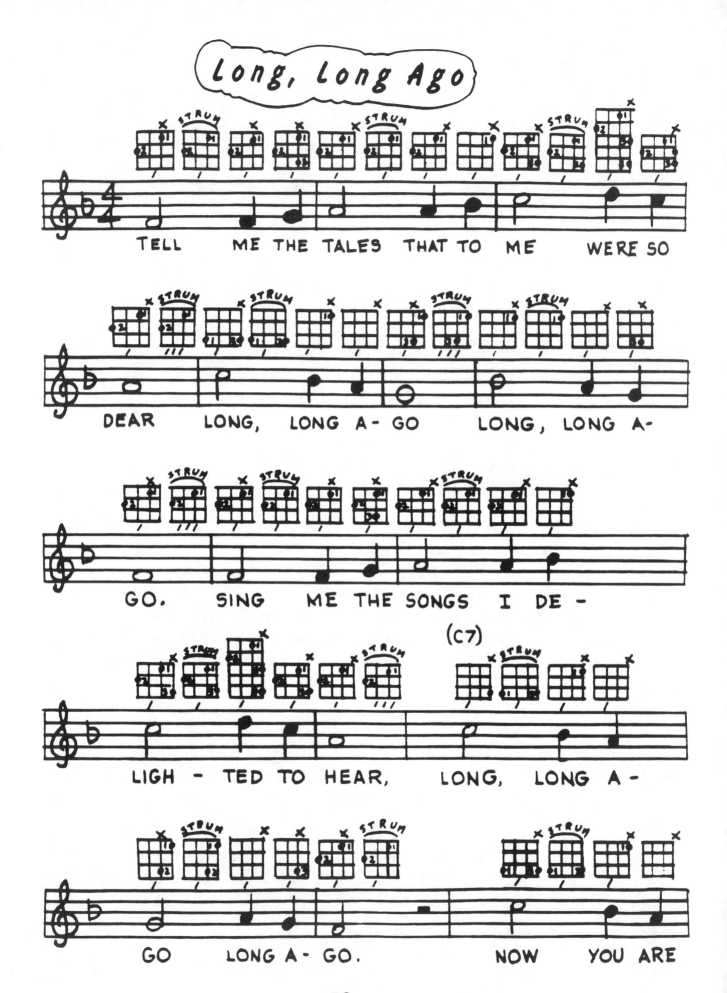

TELL ME THE TALES THAT TO ME WERE SO

DEAR LONG, LONG A-GO LONG, LONG A-

GO. SING ME THE SONGS I DE-

(C7)

LIGH-TED TO HEAR, LONG, LONG A-

GO LONG A-GO. NOW YOU ARE

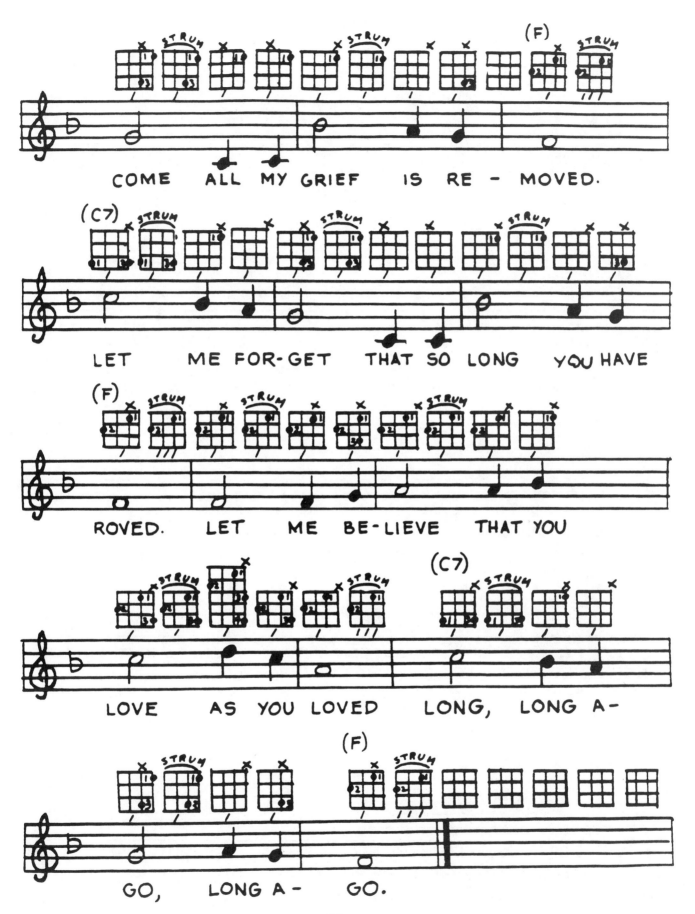

COME ALL MY GRIEF IS RE - MOVED.

LET ME FOR-GET THAT SO LONG YOU HAVE

ROVED. LET ME BE-LIEVE THAT YOU

LOVE AS YOU LOVED LONG, LONG A-

GO, LONG A - GO.

51

Strumming "Long, Long Ago" In The Key Of "F"

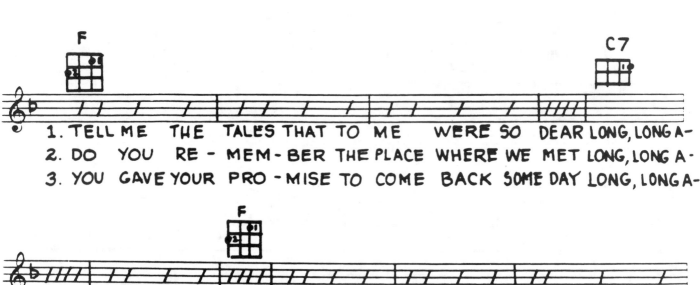

1. TELL ME THE TALES THAT TO ME WERE SO DEAR LONG, LONG A-
2. DO YOU RE - MEM - BER THE PLACE WHERE WE MET LONG, LONG A-
3. YOU GAVE YOUR PRO - MISE TO COME BACK SOME DAY LONG, LONG A-

GO, LONG, LONG A- GO. SING ME THE SONGS I DE- LIGH - TED TO
GO, LONG, LONG A- GO. AH, YES YOU TOLD ME YOU'D NE - VER FOR-
GO, LONG, LONG A- GO. THRU THE LONG WAI-TING MY HEART SEEMED TO

HEAR LONG, LONG A-GO LONG A-GO. (REST) NOW YOU ARE COME ALL MY
GET LONG, LONG A-GO LONG A-GO. THEN, TO ALL O - THERS, MY
SAY LONG, LONG A-GO LONG A-GO. NOW YOU HAVE COME ALL MY

GRIEF IS RE- MOVED. LET ME FOR-GET THAT SO LONG YOU HAVE ROVED.
SMILE YOU PRE-FERRED, LOVE, AS YOU SPOKE, GAVE A CHARM WITH EACH WORD.
GRIEF IS RE- MOVED, LET ME FOR-GET THAT SO LONG YOU HAVE ROVED.

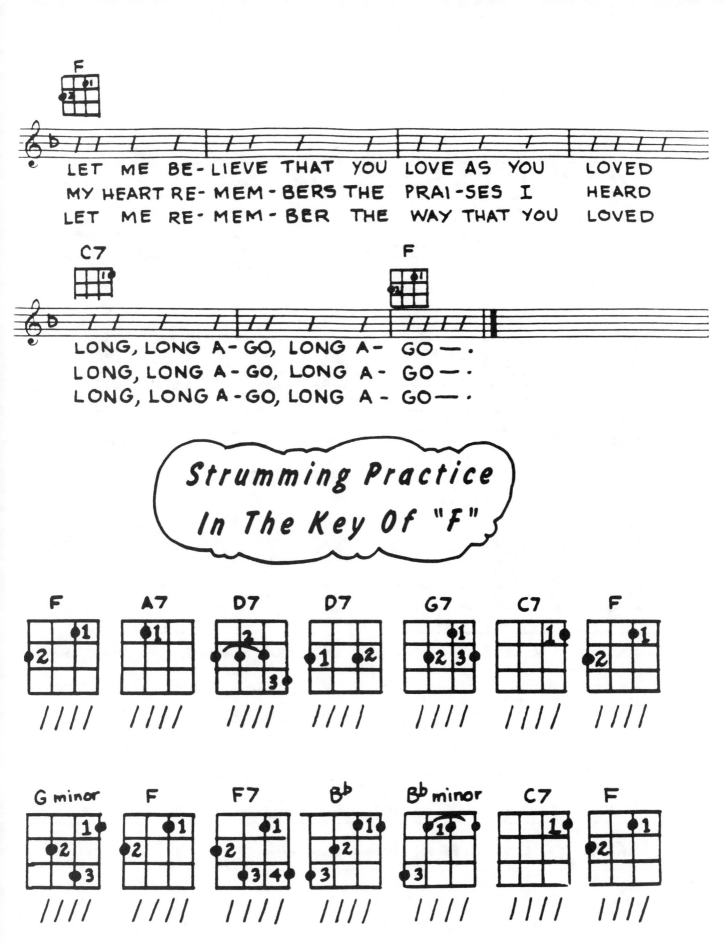

F

LET ME BE-LIEVE THAT YOU LOVE AS YOU LOVED
MY HEART RE-MEM-BERS THE PRAI-SES I HEARD
LET ME RE-MEM-BER THE WAY THAT YOU LOVED

C7　　　　　　　　　**F**

LONG, LONG A-GO, LONG A-GO—.
LONG, LONG A-GO, LONG A-GO—.
LONG, LONG A-GO, LONG A-GO—.

Strumming Practice In The Key Of "F"

F　A7　D7　D7　G7　C7　F

G minor　F　F7　Bb　Bb minor　C7　F

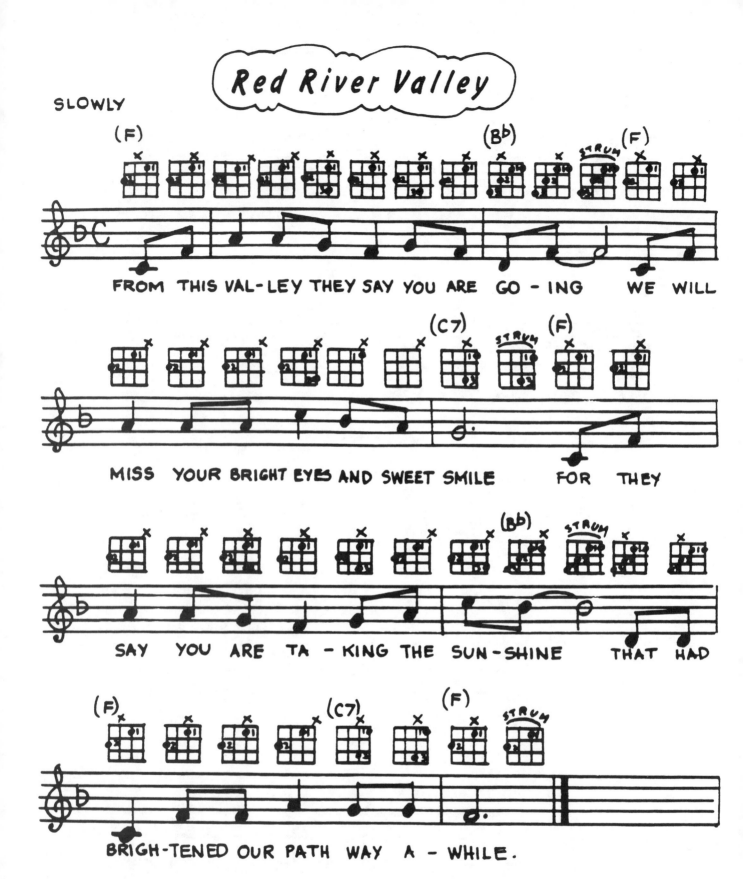

Strumming "Red River Valley"
In The Key Of "F"

F   Bb   F

1. FROM THIS VALLEY THEY SAY YOU ARE GOING WE WILL

CHORUS: COME AND SIT BY MY SIDE IF YOU LOVE ME, DO NOT

2. WON'T YOU THINK OF THE VAL-LEY YOU'RE LEAVING? OH, HOW

3. I HAVE PROMISED YOU, DAR-LING THAT NEVER WILL A

MISS YOUR BRIGHT EYES AND SWEET SMILE, FOR THEY SAY YOU ARE

(CHO.) HAS-TEN TO BID ME A-DIEU, BUT RE-MEMBER THE

LONE-LY, HOW SAD IT WILL BE, OH THINK OF THE

WORD FROM MY LIPS CAUSE YOU PAIN; AND MY LIFE IT WILL

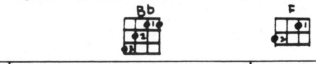

TA-KING THE SUN-SHINE THAT HAD BRIGHTENED OUR

(CHO.) RED RIVER VAL-LEY AND THE GIRL THAT HAS

FOND HEART YOU'RE BREAKING AND THE GRIEF YOU ARE

BE YOURS FOR-EVER —— IF YOU ON-LY WILL

PATH-WAY A-WHILE.

(CHO.) LOVED YOU SO TRUE.

CAU-SING ME.

LOVE ME A-GAIN.

FOLLOW SLANT (/) MARKS!

NOTE THAT THE LAST MEASURES IN THE SECOND AND THIRD ROWS HAVE ONLY TWO BEATS. THAT'S BECAUSE I RAN OUT OF SPACE. NOTICE HOW I INDICATED INCOMPLETE MEASURES WITH BROKEN STAFF LINES AT THE RIGHT.

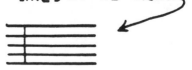

COMPLETE MEASURE (NO OPEN END)

Marines Hymn

HERE'S A GOOD PICK-STRUM CHALLENGE TO REVIEW KEY OF "C" NOTE READING:

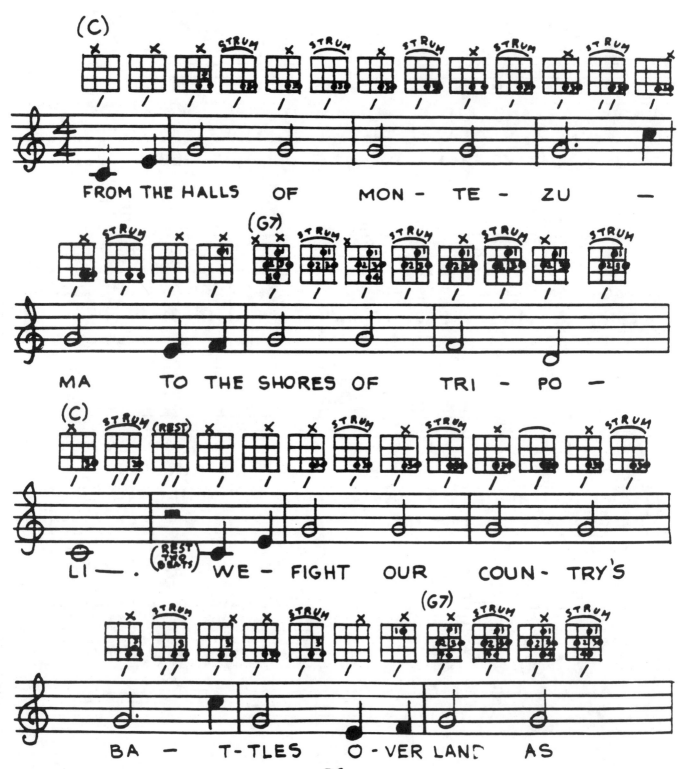

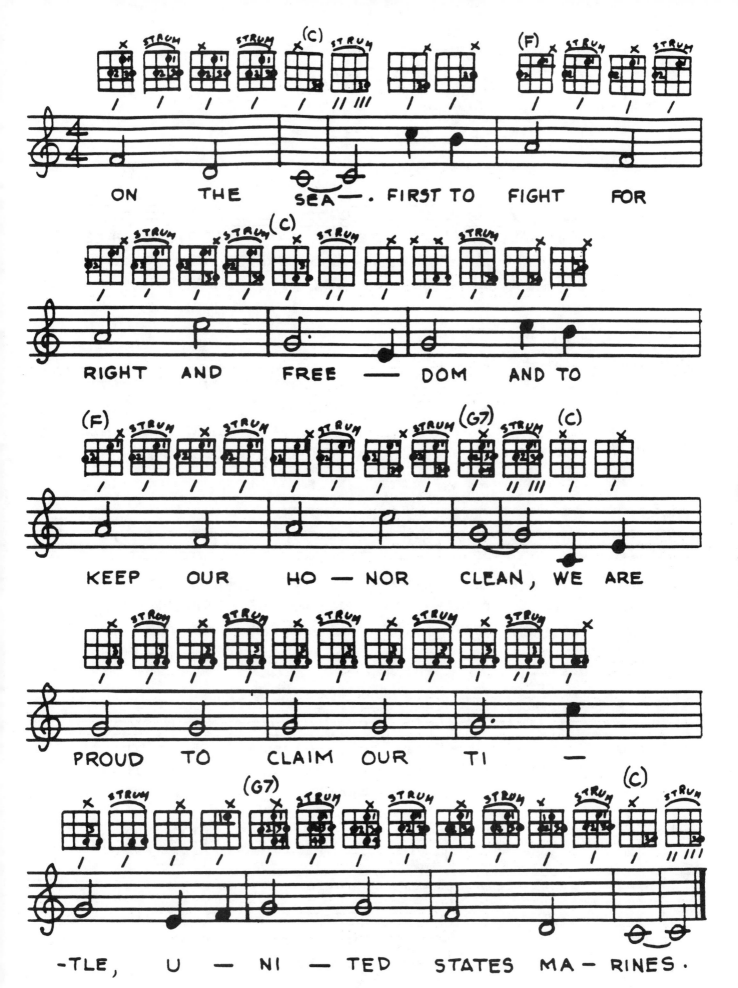

How To Do The "Tremolo"

"TREMOLO", AS THE NAME IMPLIES IS A RAPID UP-AND-DOWN PLUCKING OF A STRING OR STRINGS. (NOTE POSSIBLE WORD ASSOCIATION WITH "TREMBLING".)

WE'LL START WITH THE SINGLE STRING TREMOLO. THERE ARE TWO BASIC METHODS:

METHOD 1: THE BRACED FINGER METHOD

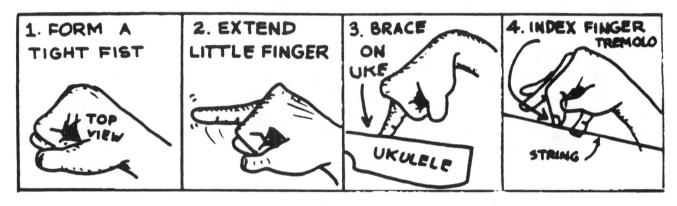

1. FORM A TIGHT FIST — TOP VIEW

2. EXTEND LITTLE FINGER

3. BRACE ON UKE — UKULELE

4. INDEX FINGER TREMOLO — STRING

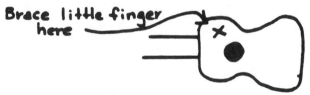

Brace little finger here

METHOD 2: THE FREE HAND SINGLE STRING METHOD

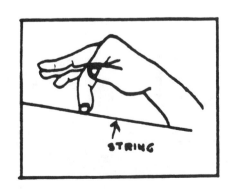

STRING

- Unlike Method 1, no bracing is used.
- Is a bit more difficult than Method 1 but well worth your practice early in your uke playing.
- Use both methods for "Daisy, Daisy".

TO BEGIN THE TREMOLO, RUN THE TIP OF YOUR
RIGHT INDEX FINGER DOWN THE STRING TO BE
TREMOLOED. IMMEDIATELY RUN THE SAME FINGER-
TIP UP ON THE SAME STRING. GO VERY SLOWLY
AT FIRST AND STRIVE FOR AN EVEN DOWN- AND-
UP MOTION. FOLLOW THE NOTES BELOW.

⊓ means downstroke
∨ means upstroke

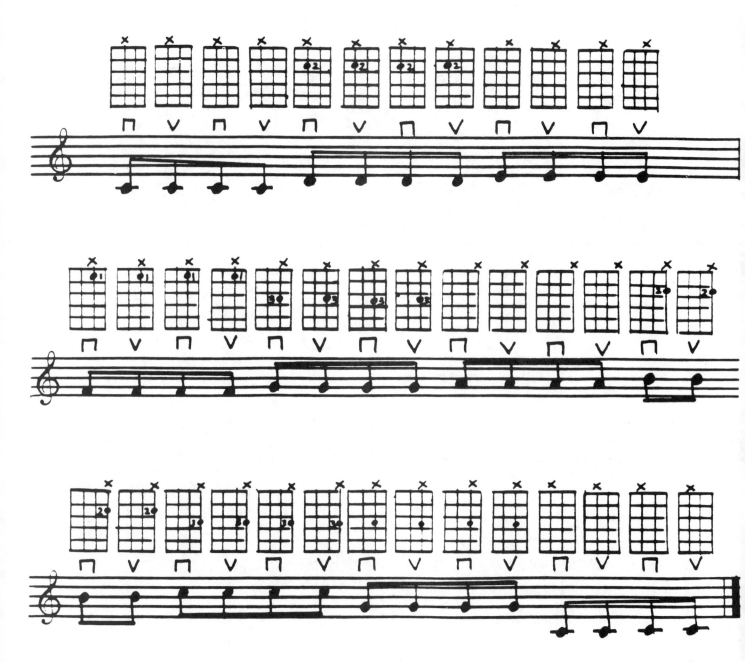

TREMOLO (CONT'D.)

THIS IS A SNEAK PREVIEW ON HOW TO PLAY THE NEXT SONG, "DAISY, DAISY".

• IN TREMOLO PLAYING, IT IS SO EASY TO LOSE TRACK OF THE BEAT OR TIMING. THUS, ESPECIALLY WHEN YOU TREMOLO, IT IS VERY IMPORTANT TO MAINTAIN A STRICT COUNT WITH YOUR FOOT.

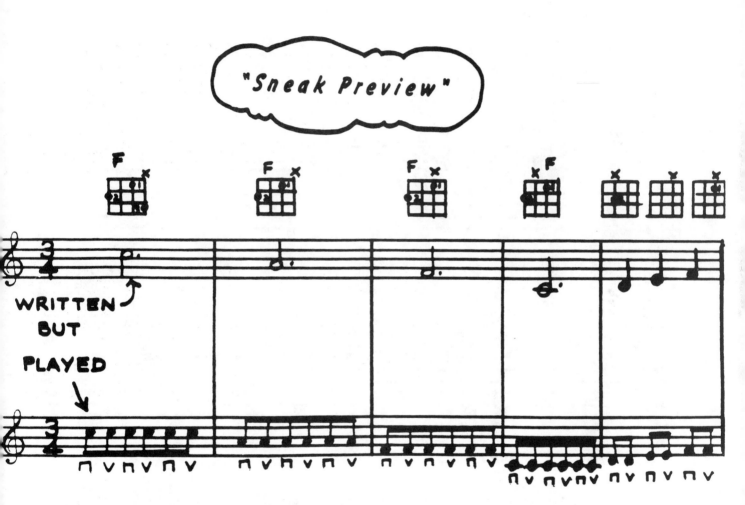

REMEMBER THAT THE EXAMPLES ARE VERY BASIC AND SLOW SPEED. ONCE YOUR TECHNIQUES IMPROVE, YOU CAN DEVELOP MORE SPEED.

Daisy, Daisy

- PLAY THIS IN REGULAR PICK-STRUM STYLE FIRST TO FAMILIARIZE YOURSELF TO THE MELODY. IF YOU HAVE TROUBLE HOLDING CHORDS WHILE PICKING SINGLE (X'ED) NOTES, JUST PICK THE "X" STRING WITHOUT THE CHORD. HOLD THE CHORD ONLY WHEN YOU COME TO A SUSTAINED NOTE FOR STRUMMING.

- FOR TREMOLO, DISREGARD THE STRUM FOR NOW. TREMOLO THE FULL VALUE OF EACH NOTE.

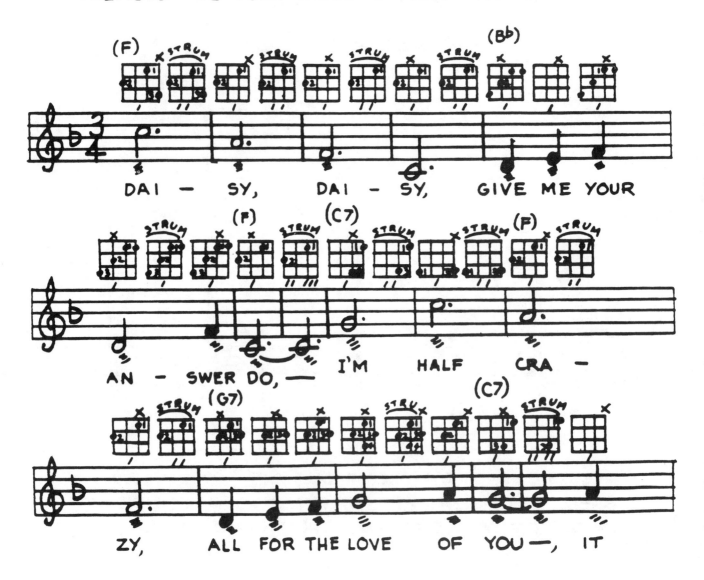

Kimura's Klosing Komments

CONGRATULATIONS IF YOU HAVE COMPLETED ALL OF THE EXERCISES AND SONGS IN THIS BOOK!

• KEEP UP YOUR PLAYING EVERY DAY, EVEN IF ONLY FOR A FEW MINUTES WHEN BUSY. SET UP A SPECIAL DAY OR DAYS EACH WEEK TO ENJOY YOUR UKE PLAYING FOR AT LEAST 30 MINUTES.

• ONCE YOU CAN PICK THE MELODY OF A SONG, SING THE WORDS TO SENSE THE RHYTHM. THEN STRUM THE CHORDS AS YOU SING THE SONG.

• AT ANY GIVEN TIME, HAVE ONE SONG YOU CAN PLAY REALLY WELL. PRACTICE IT OVER AND OVER (PICKING, STRUMMING, SINGING) UNTIL YOU CAN PLAY IT WITHOUT REFERRING TO ANY PRINTED MATERIAL. THEN IF YOU ARE SUDDENLY CALLED UPON AT A UKEFEST TO PERFORM, YOU CAN WOW 'EM WITH YOUR "PET" SONG.

• FOR THOSE OF YOU WHO ARE NOT QUITE SURE OF YOURSELF, AN AUDIO CASSETTE TAPE FOR THIS BOOK I CAN BE PURCHASED SEPARATELY. WRITE FOR CURRENT LIST OF BOOKS & TAPES.

KEEP UP THE GOOD WORK!

HAPPY UKING!

Heeday

Heeday's Ukulele Publications

94-1211-D Kipaa Place Waipahu, HI 96797